EARTH Day

by Linda Lowery
with a foreword by GAYLORD NELSON

illustrations by Mary Bergherr

Carolrhoda Books, Inc. / Minneapolis

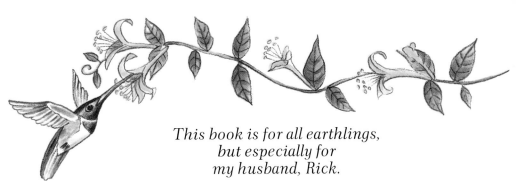

This book is for all earthlings,
but especially for
my husband, Rick.

Special thanks to former Senator Gaylord Nelson
and the Wilderness Society as well as to Denis Hayes
and Green Seal, Inc.

This book is available in two editions:
Library binding by Carolrhoda Books, Inc.
Soft cover by First Avenue Editions
241 First Avenue North
Minneapolis, MN 55401

Library of Congress Cataloging-in-Publication Data

Lowery, Linda.
    Earth Day / by Linda Lowery ; with a foreword by Gaylord Nelson ;
illustrations by Mary Bergherr.

        p. cm. — (A Carolrhoda on my own book)
    Summary: Tells the story of Earth Day 1970 and 1990 in the United
States and the special activities planned to call global attention
to the problems of pollution, environmental destruction, and waste
of natural resources.
    ISBN 0-87614-662-0 (lib. bdg.)
    ISBN 0-87614-560-8 (pbk.)
        1. Environmental policy — United States — Juvenile literature.
2. Earth Day, 1970 — Juvenile literature. 3. Earth Day, 1990 —
Juvenile literature. [1. Earth Day, 1970. 2. Earth Day, 1990.
3. Environmental protection.] I. Bergherr, Mary, ill. II. Title.
III. Series.
HC110.E5L69 1991
333.7 — dc20   90-23192
                                                                      CIP
Manufactured in the United States of America   AC

        3   4   5   6   7   8   9   10   00   99   98   97   96   95   94   93   92

Printed on recyclable,
acid-free paper.

Foreword

Who wants to breathe dirty air or swim in a polluted lake? I don't, and I'm sure you don't either.

When I was a senator, I noticed that our country's air, water, and soil were getting polluted. Plants and animals were dying. People around the United States were upset about this. They wanted to change things. But our country's leaders were not listening. They were not making laws to protect the environment.

Finally, in June of 1969, I thought of an idea to get the attention of the politicians. The idea was to have a nation-wide demonstration. I thought that if enough people got involved, everyone from the president to each city's mayor would have to take notice.

And it worked. Twenty million people came out on Earth Day 1970 and showed they cared. The politicians finally started to listen.

But that was not enough. The whole world needed to work together. So Earth Day 1990 was held. People around the planet told their government officials that they wanted action to save the Earth. And the people themselves pledged to do their part.

Now it's your chance. In not too many years, you will be the people who are running the country. What you think and do matters. So learn about nature and respect it. Live in a way that cares for the Earth. And keep after everyone from your mayor to the president to make laws that protect the planet. Your actions will make all the difference in the world.

Gaylord Nelson
founder of Earth Day
and former U.S. senator

In this huge universe,
there is one place
we can all call home.
It is the planet Earth.

Its lands are green and lively.
Its air is filled with oxygen
for us to breathe.
Everything we have
comes from the Earth—

our clothes, our food,
the homes we live in, and
the medicines that make us well.
Why not have a day
to celebrate our home,
the planet Earth?

Not long ago, a senator from
the state of Wisconsin
had that very idea.
His name was Gaylord Nelson.
During the 1960s,
Senator Nelson took many trips
across the country.
He saw Americans doing a lot of things
that harmed the planet.
They tossed litter
on the sidewalks and in the fields.
They drove their cars
as often as they could.
And their cars sent
poison gases into the air.

Farmers used chemicals on their crops
to make them grow.
The chemicals killed weeds and bugs.
The chemicals also killed
animals, fish, and birds.
Even bald eagles died.
Factories poured smoke into the skies,
turning them black.
Businesses and cities dumped trash
into lakes, rivers, and oceans.
All this spoiling of the land,
air, and water is called pollution.
Senator Nelson felt this damage
to the Earth was wrong.
He wanted the United States to make
stronger laws to stop pollution.

Then, in 1969,
something big and awful happened.
An oil well sprang a leak
near Santa Barbara, California.
Millions of tons of oil
spilled into the Pacific Ocean.

The water turned dirty and smelly.
Pelicans, egrets, sea lions,
ducks, and other animals
became coated with thick, black oil.
Most of them died.

Senator Nelson was angry.
"Something must be done to stop this!"
he told students in California.
"We are destroying the very place
we live in and love."
What can we do to wake
people up? Senator Nelson wondered.

On the plane back to Washington, D.C.,
the senator had an idea.
What if Americans set aside one day
to learn how to care
for our troubled planet?
Maybe that day could be called Earth Day.

In the next days and weeks,
Senator Nelson called everyone he knew.
He told them about his idea.
Other Americans were angry
about pollution too.
They wanted to help.
One of these people was
a law student named Denis Hayes.

Mr. Hayes said he would spend the year
helping the nation get ready
for Earth Day.
Other people offered to plan classes
and speeches in the places they lived.
Some wrote letters about pollution
to newspapers and magazines.
The word spread quickly.

On April 22, 1970,
the United States celebrated
the first Earth Day.
It was not a national holiday.
But it was the largest celebration
in Earth's history.

More than 20 million
Americans took part.
On that day, the United States Congress
did not meet.
Instead, the lawmakers went to classes
where they learned ways
to care for the Earth.

Nearly every town and school
in the nation had special activities.
Scientists, doctors, store clerks,
police officers, factory workers, teachers,
students, and others took time off
to show their concern for the Earth.
They marched.
They went to concerts.
They took nature walks and
studied about pollution.
Some people went to companies
that were polluting and asked them to stop.
In New York City,
the mayor stopped people
from driving cars on Fifth Avenue.
He wanted to show everyone how quiet
and clean the city could be.

The first Earth Day
was a great success.
People in the United States
began to litter less.
When they went to work,
they traveled together
in cars and buses.
Congress made stronger laws
and set up a new part of the government.
The new department was called the
Environmental Protection Agency (EPA).
Environment means the natural mix
of soil, water, air, climate, plants,
and animals in a certain place.
The EPA's job was to keep businesses,
cities, and states from polluting
our country's environment.

Soon the skies, the water, and
the land started to look cleaner.
More bald eagles were seen.

Ten years passed, and
Americans started to forget
the lessons of Earth Day.
They grew careless.
They began to waste
water, fuel, soil, and trees.
They acted as if these treasures
would never run out.

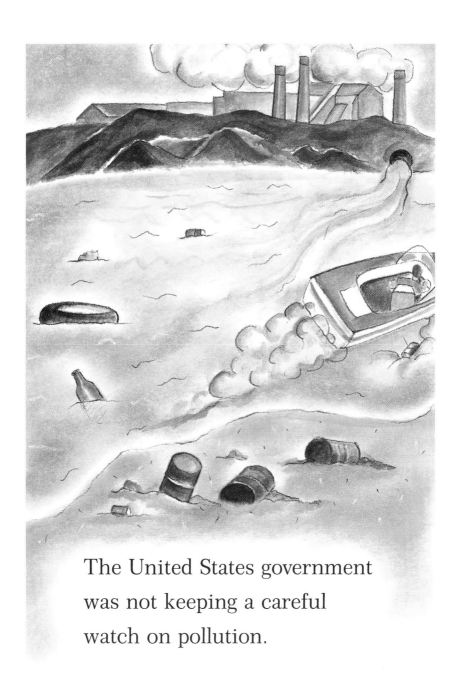

The United States government
was not keeping a careful
watch on pollution.

By now, pollution was harming more
than just the United States.
All over the planet,
poisons were quietly filling
the air, water, and land.

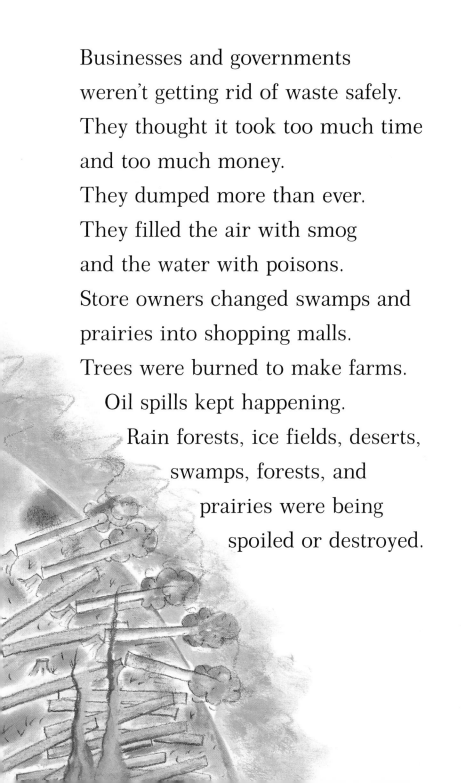

Businesses and governments
weren't getting rid of waste safely.
They thought it took too much time
and too much money.
They dumped more than ever.
They filled the air with smog
and the water with poisons.
Store owners changed swamps and
prairies into shopping malls.
Trees were burned to make farms.
   Oil spills kept happening.
      Rain forests, ice fields, deserts,
         swamps, forests, and
            prairies were being
               spoiled or destroyed.

Garbage was piling up all around.
People bought things
and used them just once.
Then they threw them away:
baby diapers, soda cans,
plastic toys, and fast-food packages.
Trucks carried the garbage
to enormous holes in the ground.

There the trash sat.
Some of it will be there forever.
Millions of acres of land
were being filled to the brim
with garbage.
And in the world's oceans,
thousands of tons of trash were floating
or had sunk to the bottom.

Creatures in every country were dying
because they had no place to live.
People were getting sick
from the poisons in the air and water.

Pollution was killing the planet,
and people were scared.
Something had to be done.

It was time for a world Earth Day.
Governments, businesses, and citizens
had to change how they were acting.
People from every nation needed
to be taught answers for
environmental problems.

For example, most garbage
can be made into new things.
This is called recycling.

People don't need to use chemicals
on their crops and lawns.
There are safer, more natural ways
to protect plants and help them grow.
Ladybugs eat many insects that eat plants.
So do birds.
And plants grow strong and healthy
in dirt made from dead plants
and food scraps.
Rain forests don't have to be burned
or cut down to be useful.
They give us rubber, fruit, nuts,
medicines, and oxygen to breathe.

Since Earth Day 1970,
Denis Hayes had been teaching
people about things such as recycling
and farming without chemicals.
He had worked to make
tougher laws to protect the water,
air, soil, and animals.
Now he decided to work on Earth Day 1990.
He called up many people
who had worked on the first Earth Day.
They all got busy again.
This time, their plans reached
far beyond the United States.

On April 22, 1990, 200 million people
in more than 140 countries
celebrated the second Earth Day.
Children around the world
formed cleanup teams.
They picked up litter
in the country and the cities.
In the United States,
T.V. programs showed what each person
could do to save the Earth.
Americans marched, sang, and
spoke out for the environment.

In Nicaragua, young people
planted 10,000 fruit trees.
Schoolchildren in Sweden visited farms
that do not use chemicals on their crops.

Japan held a Garbage Festival.
People watched while garbage
was recycled into everything
from postcards to soap.
Thousands of people joined a Litter Walk
in New Brunswick, Canada.
In Jordan, the government decided
to plant a tree for every
new baby born in the country.

A team of mountain climbers
from the United States,
the Soviet Union, and China
met at Mount Everest.
As they climbed the mountain,
they picked up the trash
others had left behind.

On Earth Day 1990,

hundreds of millions of people

worked to repair the damaged Earth.

But one day is not enough

to fix many years of harm.

People around the world

will have to change their habits for good.

If they don't,

by the time you are 30 years old,

a lot of animals and plants,

clean air and fresh water

will be gone from the Earth forever.

No one wants this to happen.
So world groups,
such as the United Nations,
are keeping up the work
of Earth Day 1990.
Even countries that have disagreed
in the past are working together.
Scientists and government leaders
are sharing ideas.
They want each country
to do these things:
cut down on garbage,
save the forests and the animals,
clean up the water and the air,
farm with fewer chemicals,
plant more trees, and
use land more wisely.

They are working to make
worldwide laws to save the Earth.
But world groups
cannot do the job alone.
Everyone must be part of the answer.
Every action we take
can help save the Earth—
or it can harm the Earth some more.
So the next time you have a can of soda pop,
will you throw the can away?
Or will you recycle it?

Earth Day happened once
in 1970 and once in 1990.
Now each April 22,
people celebrate Earth Day
in their towns, schools, and homes.
But why celebrate only once a year?
We can do better than that.
We can make every day an Earth Day.
If we do our share each day,
we WILL save the planet.
After all, the Earth is
the only home we have.
It can't wait.
Can we?

At Home

Reuse things.
Used things are cheaper and have that nice broken-in feel. Give your used toys and clothes to other children, so they can enjoy them too.

Make new soil.
With help from an adult, mix fruit and vegetable scraps with leaves, grass, and twigs. Put them in a wire basket or special wooden box and let them sit outside. This is called composting. In the spring, the new soil can go in your garden or window box.

Recycle garbage.
Save newspapers, cans, and bottles. If your city doesn't pick up recyclables, call your city council or government offices and ask who does. Find out if plastic things are recycled in your area.

Save energy.
Turn off the lights and the T.V. set when you leave a room.

Plant trees.
Each tree cleans the air and makes new oxygen for us to breathe. It gives animals and insects places to make homes.

OFF

Can Make
EARTH DAY

Buy toys that will last.
Try to choose things that will not break easily and that you will like for a long time.

Help save the rain forests.
Buy ice cream and candy made with rain-forest fruit and nuts, such as figs and cashews. If people can make money selling fruit and nuts from the rain forests, they will save the forests' trees.

Save trees and cut down on garbage.
At picnics and parties, use cloth napkins, metal forks and knives, and reusable plates. They are better for the planet than those made of plastic or paper.

Do not make garbage.
Buy toys and snack foods that are not packed in Styrofoam, plastic wrap, or shiny, printed paper. These wrappings are not recyclable.

Learn about nature.
Visit parks, wildlife centers, and nature reserves. Read books and watch T.V. programs on animals, plants, birds, fish, and insects.

Respect our environment.
Remember that animals, insects, streams, wildflowers, grass, air, people, soil, and forests all depend on each other. So don't squash bugs, don't tease animals, and don't litter.

At School

Save energy and cut down on harmful gases in the air.
Instead of asking someone to drive you to school (or other places), walk, ride your bike, take the bus, or ride with friends.

Save trees.
If you use both sides of your art or notebook paper, fewer trees need to be cut to make more paper.
If you buy recycled paper, you save even more trees. You can even ask your principal not to have paper cups and plates (as well as plastic or foam utensils) used in the cafeteria.

Help to make stronger laws to protect the environment.
Send letters to your mayor and city council members, to your county and state officials. (Your teachers have their names and addresses.) Tell them that you want laws to support recycling, to stop pollution, to save animals, and to protect the places in which animals live. You can even send a letter to the president.
Here is the address:

The White House
1600 Pennsylvania Avenue
Washington, D C 20500

For more information on what you and your friends or classmates can do, write to these groups:

The Children's Rainforest
P. O. Box 936
Lewiston, ME 04240

Global ReLeaf c/o
American Forestry Assoc.
P. O. Box 2000
Department WM
Washington, DC 20013

Green Seal, Inc.
P.O. 1694
Palo Alto, CA 94302

Kids Against Pollution
c/o Tenakill School
275 High Street
Closter, NJ 07624

Save Our Streams Prog.
c/o Izaak Walton
League of America
1401 Wilson Boulevard
Level B
Arlington, VA 22209